The BOOK of JONES

Entrance to Owl Farm Woody c

Ralph STEADman

The BOOK of JONES

Home of JONES.

HARCOURT BRACE & COMPANY   New York   San Diego   London

To Laila Nabulsi,
beauty to the beasts

Copyright © 1997, 1995 by Ralph Steadman

First published in the United Kingdom in 1995 by
Ebury Press, Random House, 20 Vauxhall Bridge Road,
London SW1V 2SA

Library of Congress Cataloging-in-Publication Data
Steadman, Ralph.
The book of Jones/Ralph Steadman.—1st U.S. ed.
p. cm.
ISBN 0-15-100309-2
1. Cats—Caricatures and cartoons. 2. English wit
and humor, Pictorial. I. Title.
NC1479.S79A4 1997
741.5'942—dc21 97-23665

Text set in Weiss
Designed by Lori McThomas Buley
Printed in the United States of America
First U.S. edition
ABCDE

Jones wants to come in.

If I had really wanted to do a book about cats, I would have done it years ago. But Jones is dead, and if ever a cat should be remembered, it's Jones. I only met him the once, for just two weeks, but in that time he left a deep impression.

I was staying at Woody Creek, Colorado, as a guest of the writer Hunter S. Thompson, my collaborator on many maverick assignments.

With his lovely girlfriend, Laila Nabulsi, we found
ourselves the victims of a book we were trying to
lash together, *The Curse of Lono*, and the curse was fast
overtaking our efforts. But that's what acts of creation
are all about: like childbirth, there are spasms of pain,
periods of inertia, contractions and then, if you're
lucky, some kind of offspring,
with its father's eyes
and a mother's smile.

Tomas's Seat

Jones on The Carpet

Hunter had kept other animals over
the years, chosen—like any pet—impulsively
and from what was available at the time.
But Jones chose Hunter, or at least Hunter's
house. It suited his purpose right down to
the tip of his bushy tail.

The only creatures in the house likely to give Jones any competition for affection were Hunter's peacocks, but they were too bizarre to put up a challenge. Jones just let them be, smart cat that he was. Anyway, there were five of them, and even one is too many if you want to wring its bloody neck.

Jones and Hunter's
Peacock S.

Jones weighs up a Peacock

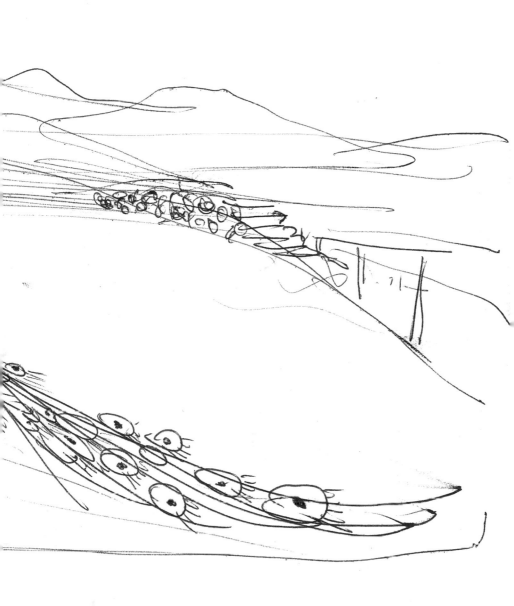

So Jones stayed and, by the looks of things when I showed up, very much on his own terms. He and his master shared a deep and guarded respect, a kind of mutual recognition of each other's stealth in matters of survival.

It was Laila who fed them both, and each in his strange way was treated like a pet in need of special treatment. Both made demands and were locked into worlds reserved for selfish gods. Nobody could complain about that since terms of existence, wherever gods find themselves, are absolute. Personally, I accept the general pattern of daily life, no matter how weird, as normal. Otherwise, how do you survive?

Jones
on his
pedéstal.

Jones in luck.

Jones being
Lifted.

Perhaps only a cat would try something strange and against the grain while purring softly, arching the back, and rubbing itself enticingly against your leg. Which is why a cat can get away with it.

Jones in torment

Cats have been known to smother babies in cribs out of pure love of comfort and warmth, then curl themselves around people's legs in search of nothing more than praise. They are the personification of evil; yet they can do no wrong. They exist, utterly themselves, and, no matter how fierce the storm raging around them, find the warmest place to be.

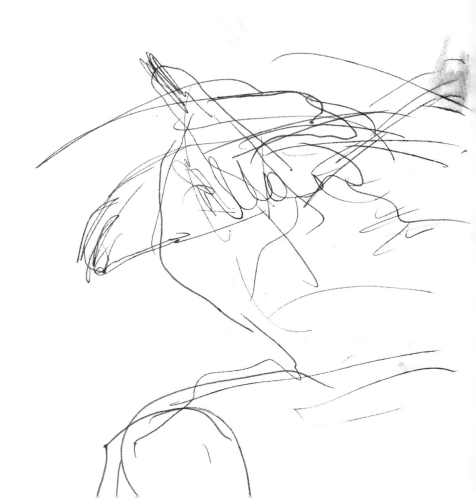

Jones turns
a cold
shoulder.

I have never met a cat more insolent and yet more appealing than Jones. He never needed to judge a situation; he *was* the situation. It took me two days to feel the full weight of his authority, and when I did, I decided to buy a handsome sketchbook from a store in Aspen. I wanted to try to catch something of his arch presence. God knows, I'm not much of an animal person—at home I try to cope with three sheep and one tiny rabbit, and so far I have three bags of wool and a ton of rabbit shit.

2-second Jones.

One-way Jones.

Emotions depend on your frame of mind at a particular time. Even a cathedral is simply a bunch of big stones if you are feeling bloody-minded. Maybe Jones filled an empty space majestically at the right moment. He inspired veneration like the leader of a new cult.

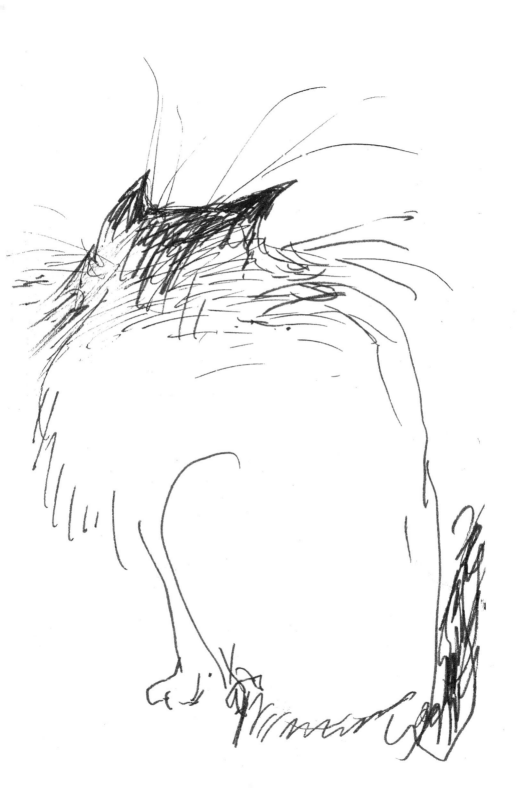

Jones
plays
God.

I am trying to remember when I first caught a particularly virulent dose of Jones's clawed charm. . . . His fur swelled from his cheeks like a display of carnival fireworks, but he wasn't smiling at me; he was drawing from within himself the unbearable pleasures of his own world. His acknowledgment was nothing more than a passing reflection on my existence, as a possible source of some other diversion he had not yet thought of. He had no other use for me.

A touch of Jones.

What the hell! The world needs creatures like
Jones to remind us that we are selfish too. If you think
you are a saint, try to prove it; you will not be loved
for doing so.

Jones gave everything he had to himself without burning so much as a calorie. In the valleys of his mind he sunbathed as he waited for the sun to go down. When it did, his real life began. He came out from behind the veil of his myopic lethargy and began to play.

Jones watches the
Sun go down

Some cats play like kittens. They display the boundless energy of the newborn. They are coy and self-conscious, but eager for a confrontation. They fall on their backs and tumble like autumn leaves. Eyes bright with anticipation, jaws wide open, they show and contemplate their vulnerable underbellies. Then, suddenly, they are up and at you with the instincts of lions but the strength of babies.

Jones growls softly.

Jones guarding
his territory

Jones would have none of that. He played like a bored Roman emperor tolerating the entertainment offered up by gladiators and Christians. He had seen it all before.

Jones allowed you to make the first move and watched languidly as you did so. He would lie like an eagle's wing across a couch, and the last thing on his mind was play, least of all with someone other than himself, and certainly not with a stranger.

Foolishly, you ruffle the fur on his exposed stomach; it is so soft and inviting. People have common ways of saying "No" to advances, but a cat has to use a wordless gesture to ward off an unwanted playful lunge.

Jones knew what to do at once. One savage paw on the back of my hand was all the discouragement I needed. I quickly learned when it was wrong to cross Jones. He would not tolerate mindless stupidity, which is probably why Hunter and he understood each other so well.

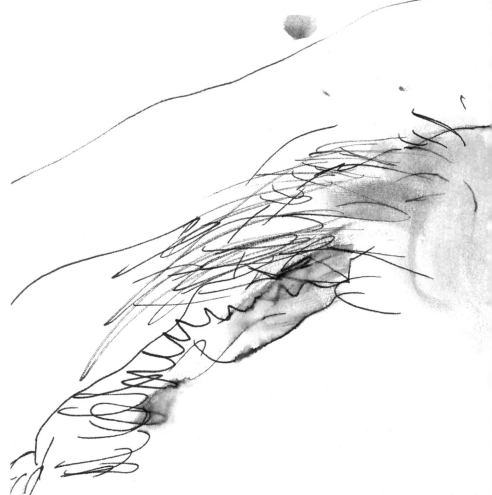

He could, however, adopt a pathetic, pleading demeanor whenever he wanted something that required your indulgence, such as opening the door onto the rolling outdoors of his domain. But if his patience was stretched by a momentary hesitation on your part, he would growl gently for immediate action. Those were the very times when his appeal was irresistible, causing a great surge of love and admiration to fan my creative fires.

I needed to capture some of these moments, and the best way I know is with a few direct lines, straight from the eye through the mind to the hand. The result on paper can be fiendishly perceptive or hopelessly inaccurate, but it is always an intriguing and playful possibility.

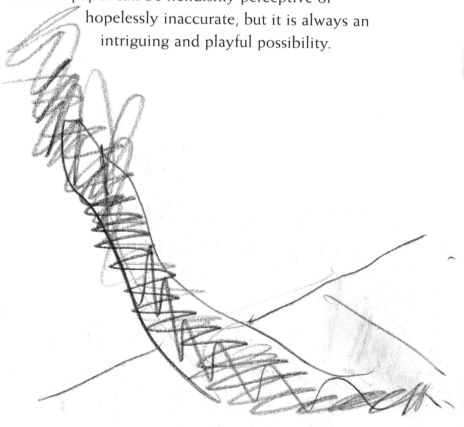

Jones in
Trafalgar
Square.

Drawing often has this power, which may account for the intense interest shown when anyone makes an impression on paper. No matter how pedestrian the result, we feel that something mysterious and rare has happened within a private world, and we are privileged to witness it in this vague and doubtful revelation.

In my drawings, Jones decided the style and I went along with it, being the weaker of the two parties. Jones had a manner which engaged many people. His remoteness was a spur rather than a hindrance to natural affinity. He found his place and knew it. He coveted nothing but his own comfort, and lacked only a god's control over his own fate.

Jones thinking

My drawings are a scrambled response—the grabbing of a sketch pad, the frantic search for the pen or chalk at the knife-edge moment when Jones had come to rest in an attitude of high condescension, the outward manifestation of a flitting mood or of his brooding inner spirit. They are nearly cartoons, but essentially my serious attempt to capture the finer artistry of Jones's posture, and often merely a wisp of memory registered by the eye as he floated through my gaze. Our close detachment came about because we were often the only ones awake. Since Hunter's habits and activities are nocturnal, the rest of the household slept the early part of the day away.

Jones thinking
some more

On many nights I struggled to stay up so we could work together, but I still needed to go to bed during the dark hours. I find it impossible to sleep without guilt when the day has come. Perhaps it is my Welsh mining ancestry on my mother's side. Honest work is a daily activity which begins with the coming of light. The night is for sleeping and private acts of creation.

So I would stalk the house all day between fitful
bursts of drawing for *The Curse of Lono*, seemingly alone
with the muted sounds of peacocks on the balcony
outside, the electric hum of the stereo equipment

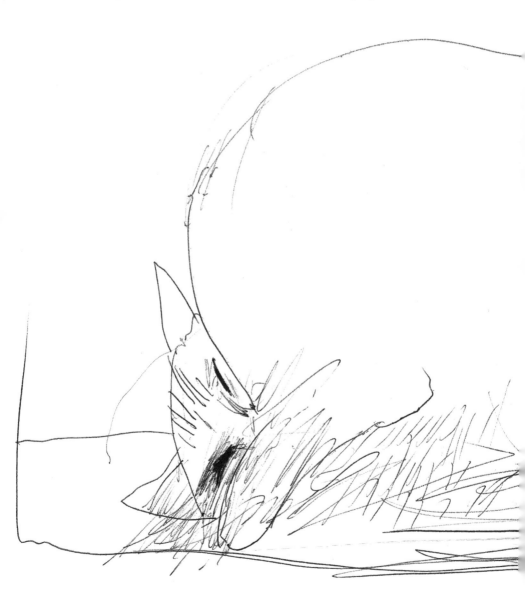

and the hiccuping fridge, the raucous burst of an occa-
sional phone call feeding the answering machine, and
the purring of Jones as he wallowed through the
trough of the day. . . .

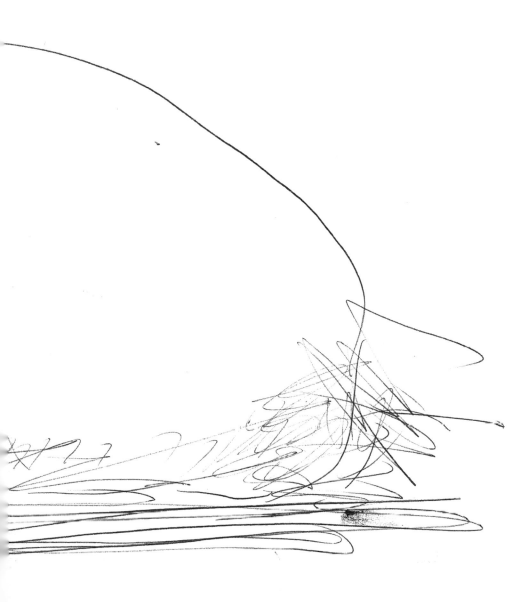

The early autumn colors of change gently tinted the old log cabin ambiance, and a cooler sun broke into the house like blocks of glowing ice, illuminating a corner and shedding a reflected light over the couch where Jones lay haloed—and I watched. Maybe he would look in my direction through a haze of half-closed shimmering eyelash eyes with an unerring appreciation of his own smug self-satisfaction.

Then, as though a meandering thought of some previous engagement pricked his bubble mind, with swift stealth he was seated by the door, throwing back at me his imploring look before it froze into a stony glare and elicited my dutiful response.
Thy will be done.

And so it was.

Sour
Puss!
Jones.

In those two weeks, odd friends came and went, stayed and dabbled, made arrangements, laughed and ate, slept on sofas. The actor John Belushi tumbled through on one weekend, reeking of fatigue and rocket-fuel adrenaline. He buried his face in cushions as if burrowing in search of relief from his bruised brilliance. Frenetic outbursts burned him up like a Roman candle.

Jones treated him and the rest with similar détente. Everyone was a moving thing to tease his whim with respect and worship at the altar he had made his own. No one meant more than that, for somewhere in his mysterious past, there gnawed a faceless memory; perhaps a thoughtless indiscretion when he had given all his love and trust to such a moving thing as those who surrounded him now. Maybe it was a tragic disappointment and he had learned, as much by instinct as by guile, that where he stood was all he could expect, and thereby laid his claim.

One of
Jones's friends:
John
Belushi

Then I, like all the others, left. For all Jones cared, we might never have met. I was just another passing entertainment.

Later, Laila came to visit me in England. "How's Jones?" I asked.

"Jones is dead," she told me. "And that's how I heard it. Just like that." She had phoned Hunter, and asked, as I did, "How's Jones?" He struggled to tell her gently, but hesitant explanations merely triggered the desire to get it over with, and the truth tumbled out abruptly. "He's dead. JONES IS DEAD!"

Laila told me how he died, but I forget and maybe I don't really want to know. Perhaps I will ask Hunter the next time I see him. . . .

Jones on the other side.